HEIDEGGER IN 90 MINUTES

Heidegger
IN 90 MINUTES

Paul Strathern

IVAN R. DEE
CHICAGO

Library of Congress Cataloging-in-Publication Data:
Strathern, Paul, 1940–
    Heidegger in 90 minutes / Paul Strathern.
      p. cm.
    Includes bibliographical references and index.
    ISBN 1-56663-439-3 (alk. paper) — ISBN 1-56663-438-5 (pbk. : alk. paper)
    1. Heidegger, Martin, 1889–1976.   I. Title: Heidegger in ninety minutes.   II. Title.
B3279.H49 S76 2002
193—dc21   2002019505

Contents

HEIDEGGER IN 90 MINUTES

Introduction

Heidegger may have been the most controversial philosopher of the twentieth century. During the first half of that century the course of philosophy diverged as never before. There became, in fact, *two* philosophical traditions. These proved so incompatible that no discourse was possible between them. One regarded the other as sheer nonsense. The other regarded the former as having entirely missed the point of philosophy. Any reconciliation was out of the question.

On the one hand was the philosophy of linguistic analysis, which derived largely from Wittgenstein. As its name suggests, this philosophy required extreme rigor in the use of words. Philosophical problems were deemed to arise from the misapplication of words. In such cases, a word was used in a context to which it could not apply—which resulted in the "knot" of a problem. As soon as the knot was untangled by suitable analysis, the problem simply vanished. For instance, take the question: "What is the meaning of existence?" This was a question that simply *could not be asked.* And why not? Because to apply the term "meaning" to the term "existence" was invalid. For existence to have a meaning, this meaning would somehow have to exist above and beyond existence. But it is impossible for something to exist *outside* existence. Just as it is impossible for something to be red that is not red, true that is not true. Such analysis explains why there can be no answer to the question: "What is the meaning of existence?"

The other tradition of philosophy, which derived from Heidegger, was diametrically opposed to such analysis. Indeed, its fundamental question was: "What is being?" In other words, "What does it mean to exist?" or "What is the meaning of existence?" For Heidegger and the existential tradition, this question could not simply be "analyzed away." Such questions were beyond the reach of logic or reason. They lay deeper. Our existence was fundamental: prior to rational thought or linguistic analysis. It was the primary "given" of every individual life.

In order to ask such questions about being, about existence, an entire new form of philosophy had to be developed. This was what Heidegger saw as his lifelong task.

Heidegger's Life and Works

Martin Heidegger was born on September 26, 1889, in the south German mountain village of Messkirch, just a dozen miles north of Lake Constance and the border with Switzerland. This was a pious rural area, where little had changed for centuries. Heidegger came from a background of small farmers and craftsmen. His father was a master cooper and sexton of the local Catholic church, his mother a farmer's daughter from a neighboring village. Martin showed an early interest in religion and seemed destined to join the priesthood. After high school he became a Jesuit novice, going to Freiburg University on a church scholarship in 1909 to study theology.

But soon it became clear to him that his main interest was in philosophy, and after two years he switched to this subject. This was a brave decision, as it meant that he lost his church scholarship. But it was already evident to the university authorities that he had exceptional talent. He was given a small grant, which he supplemented by private tutoring.

In Heidegger's school years there are no tales of escapades or the usual scrapes in which students become involved. Young Martin was intensely preoccupied with spiritual-philosophical questions. The earnest country boy was deeply unsettled by the manifestations of the modern urban world that he encountered in Freiburg. This may have been an out-of-the way provincial city, but the nearby Black Forest attracted a constant stream of cosmopolitan tourists. The citizens and students of Freiburg prided themselves on keeping up with the latest intellectual and social trends which were sweeping Germany. During the 1890s and 1900s the country was undergoing an astonishing transformation into a major industrial power. When German unification culminated in the founding of the German Empire in 1871, 70 percent of its population had been living on the land; by 1910 this had fallen to 40 percent. The old traditional rural Germany in which Heidegger had grown up had remained largely undisturbed since medieval times. Now it was giving way to modern cities where automobiles, electrification, and heavy industry prevailed. All aspects of Western culture were becoming urbanized.

Philosophy too was undergoing an analogous crisis. Since the beginning of the nineteenth century, Germany had prided itself on providing the leading European philosophers, such as Kant and Hegel. They had produced all-embracing metaphysical systems which explained the world and everything in it, including humanity. In many ways these systems had begun to take the place of God. (It was Hegel, not Nietzsche, who first pronounced "God is dead.") Such systems were a way of viewing how the world worked. They were grounded in metaphysics—that is, in beliefs and assumptions that lay beyond our experience of the physical world. (Metaphysics literally means "beyond physics.") But the tradition of grand and immensely serious metaphysical systems like those conceived by Kant, Hegel, and even Schopenhauer had come to an end. Gleefully Nietzsche had exploded this inflated tradition of systematic philosophy with pinpricks of epigrammatic wit before scandalously dying of syphilitic insanity in 1900. For Hegel, "God is dead" had been an insight; for Nietzsche it was the basis of his entire philosophy.

Since then the preeminence of philosophy had been undermined by science and its new sibling subject, psychology. (There is an illuminating analogy here between the contemporaneous process of art being undermined by photography.) For many, scientific truth had begun to supplant philosophic truth. In 1905 Einstein had produced his Special Theory of Relativity. In this, the long-standing philosophical problem of time was simply reduced to the fourth dimension in the space-time continuum. Philosophy had become mathematics. Worse was to come with quantum theory, also described by Einstein in 1905, where light could be regarded as both a particle and a wave. In other words, light was solid matter and an immaterial motion *simultaneously*. Scientific reality defied the basic rule of logic: the law of contradiction. (An entity is something, or it is not something: it cannot be both at the same time, or neither.) The entire notion of philosophy was based upon logic.

Many, including Einstein himself, saw this illogicality as just a temporary anomaly, which would soon be resolved. It was nothing more than a necessary mathematical sleight of hand needed to overcome apparently conflicting experimental evidence. After all, mathematics too surely depended upon logic.

Yet even if logic survived this onslaught, it faced another threat—this time from psychology. According to "psychologism," as it came to be called, logic was not based upon universal rules, and thus it did not produce abstract irrefutable truths. As early as 1865 the English philosopher John Stuart Mill had declared that logic in fact "owes all its theoretical foundations to psychology." The truths of psychology initially arose from self-observation and our personal experience of the world. This meant that the axioms upon which we base our thought must surely be no more than "generalizations from experience." The law of contradiction was not a universal truth, it was simply the way human beings thought. Logic was rooted in our psychology. So what became of philosophy? Was our entire attempt to know the truth about ourselves and the world doomed?

The twenty-two-year-old Heidegger had turned to philosophy in order to reach beyond all that he found inadequate in theology. He had wished to discover a certainty in which to ground his resistance to all the bewildering and multiplying uncertainties of the modern urban technological world. But now even philosophy itself was coming to an accommodation with science and modernity. The trend was away from the lofty spirituality he sought, toward down-to-earth positivism. This attempted to eliminate all systems and remnants of metaphysics from philosophy. Only truths such as those of experience, scientific experiment, or mathematics were acceptable. All of these could be either demonstrated or proved.

The main modern philosophy that sought to resist this trend was phenomenology, whose leading exponent was the German philosopher Edmund Husserl. Early in his student days, Heidegger borrowed Husserl's *Logical Investigations* from the university library. Reading this work proved nothing less than a revelation to him. He kept the book in his room for the next two years. (Evidently no one asked for it at the library.) Heidegger was so overwhelmed that he "read it again and again." He even became obsessed with the physical actuality of the book itself: "The spell emanating from the work extended to the outer appearance of the sentence structure and the title page."

Heidegger graduated in 1913 but continued with postgraduate studies at Freiburg. A year later Europe was plunged into a world war. This traumatic event was at first welcomed with almost universal enthusiasm. On both sides, thousands of young men rushed to volunteer. Columns of troops marching to the railway stations to embark for the front were pelted with flowers by cheering crowds—from Glasgow to Budapest, from St. Petersburg to Rome. Many, of all classes, who had sensed an emptiness in their lives, now found a meaning in emotional patriotism. But this was to be a war without glory, such as none had foreseen. Battle tactics as ancient as battle itself were used against modern weapons. Machine guns mowed down advancing lines of thousands upon thousands, gas warfare blinded and suffocated, entire resentful armies rotted in the mud of the trenches. The civilian population was kept largely oblivious of this, with life continuing as before. Meanwhile an entire era of class-stratified society, inspired by the certainties of "God and country," formed by "a century of peace, progress, and prosperity," was dying amidst a slaughter the like of which had never been seen before. (On the opening day of the Battle of the Somme there were almost sixty thousand casualties, a figure similar to the results when the first atomic bomb was dropped on Hiroshima forty years later. The Battle of the Somme would continue for another *four and a half months*.)

Heidegger was called to military service but found to have a weak heart. He was placed in the reserves and ended up back in Freiburg working as a mail censor, a cushy job which enabled him to continue with his philosophy. In 1915 he began teaching at the university. The twenty-six-year-old from the backwoods had now become a university lecturer embarking upon a respectable career, with high prospects. Though earnest and "spiritual," he was also highly ambitious. In 1916 he became engaged to Elfride Petri, an independently minded economics student who came from a Prussian military family. Three months later they were married. By this time the famous Husserl had arrived as professor of philosophy at Freiburg, and Heidegger had become his assistant. Although phenomenology was hardly well known outside academic circles, it was already being seen as something more than just a new philosophy. This was a movement that might one day fill the "spiritual vacuum" that many were beginning to discern at the heart of German culture. Such was Heidegger's deep and perceptive understanding of Husserl's phenomenology that the two quickly became close. The professor soon began looking upon his bright young assistant in recognizably paternal terms. Here perhaps was his eventual successor in the growing phenomenological movement.

Husserl was convinced that he had found the answer to "psychologism" as well as to positivism's attempt to reduce all "truth" to scientific truth. It was not a matter of denying such claims but attacking them head-on. According to his analysis, such views might be true within their own realm, but they remained ultimately inadequate. Science and psychology were based upon experiments, which meant that they always remained to a certain extent inexact, unlike the precise truths of logic and mathematics. $2+2=4$ *precisely.* There is not even a possibility that it might just be 4.000001: we know that even to a thousandth of a percent and beyond it is always correct. Compare this with the most precise measurements of the speed of light, which can now be calculated to well within a millionth of a percent. We accept the value of this constant as 186,000 miles per second, but we know that this can never be exactly correct, no matter how precise our measurements. Here Husserl was in

20

agreement with Einstein, who maintained: "As far as the laws of mathematics refer to reality, they are not certain, and as far as they are certain, they do not refer to reality."

For Husserl, the laws of mathematics were ideal, they existed a priori—that is to say, they existed before our experience, and regardless of our experience. Even if there were no human beings to experience it, two plus two would still equal four. There remained a categorical difference between these ideal laws and real laws (those we apprehend in reality). Admittedly, we first become aware of these ideal laws by experience. But a logical or mathematical law is not confirmed by any "feeling" we may have when we experience it. We intuit it, and at once we realize that it is self-evident. When we see that 2+2=4, we somehow know it is true.

If psychologism was correct, this would mean that 2+2=4 would not be incontrovertible. It would simply arise from one's personal intuition of the world. Others might intuit it differently—and we would have no grounds for refuting them.

Husserl used the example of geometry, which

he considered the most absolute and incontrovertible of all mathematical knowledge. The entire edifice of geometry was built upon a foundation that consisted of such basic concepts as "line," "distance," "point," and so forth. According to Husserl, there was certainly an actual day in prehistoric time when particular individuals must have had intuitions of these concepts. In the midst of the flow of his experience, a particular primitive human being suddenly intuited the idea of a "point." Later, another understood the concept of "line." But once understood, these concepts had a precise and undeniable meaning. The rest of geometry consisted simply of exploring the logical implications that arose from these basic concepts. For instance, if we have one line, it is possible to have two lines, or even three. If these three lines are joined so as to enclose a space, they will form a figure with three angles: a triangle. This is necessarily true, and *could not be otherwise*. It had always been true, and always would be. Geometry did not contain these truths, they were "already there," simply waiting to be discovered. This was the same with all mathematics, all logic, all absolute knowledge. They somehow existed beyond reality, beyond the inexactitudes and uncertainties of everyday life. They existed in a realm of their own. There was a "presence" where absolute truth existed—the only alternative would have been an "absence." Such a "presence" guaranteed all absolute truth by its very existence.

Husserl's "presence" bears a strong resemblance to an unseen all-seeing God, whose existence guarantees all truth. Indeed, at the outset of his career Husserl had stated that his aim was "to find the way to God and to a truthful life through strict philosophical scholarship."

But to find this way by philosophical means it was necessary to study the one subject whose truth was closest to us—namely ourselves, humanity itself. Here too there was a similar division between the uncertainties of reality and absolute truth. In Husserl's view, the essential study of humanity, the true subject of philosophy, lay far beyond the reach of science or psychology. His phenomenology proposed a "philosophy of Absolute Being" which arose in a "universally true" consciousness. Here was where philosophy originated, beyond even the need for any fundamental presuppositions, such as were required by logic. Here was the ultimate philosophy, which existed of its own accord. But how was it possible to reach this "pure" and "universally true" consciousness? Evidently this was not possible by means of scientific or even logical methods. It could only be achieved by using a phenomenological approach that Husserl called "reduction."

Reduction involved concentrating upon consciousness and eliminating any attention to particulars by "bracketing them out." In this way one would be left with pure consciousness, with the "essential, universal structure of the mind." First, one "bracketed out" reality. As Husserl pointed out, reality consists of real objects, but these objects are not objects in consciousness itself. They exist outside consciousness in the real world—where they are best studied by scientific means. Second, it was necessary to "bracket out" the objects and acts of consciousness itself. As we have seen, these objects were not the ob-

24

jects of reality itself, they were representations of this reality. They appeared in our consciousness through acts of consciousness, such as memory and perception. Similar acts of consciousness included judging, analyzing, contemplating, and so forth. These too could be "bracketed out." We are then left with consciousness itself—"pure" consciousness—the unifying realm where all our awareness takes place. At this point we experience the "origin-immune" truth of our "primal givenness" (in the sense that awareness is given to us). In this way we are aware of a "transcendental ego" which is "universally true" and is thus part of an "Absolute Being."

Heidegger initially accepted Husserl's analysis but soon began to modify it with ideas of his own. This would be the beginning of his original philosophy—nonetheless it would remain heavily indebted to Husserl's phenomenological approach.

In 1918 Heidegger was called up and dispatched to a meteorological unit outside Sedan in German-occupied eastern France. By now the German army was beginning to disintegrate as the Allies advanced. Heidegger took part in no actual fighting but was deeply affected by the historical events unfolding around him. In rapid succession the kaiser abdicated and fled to Holland, Germany became a republic under a Social Democratic government, and the German army surrendered. A humiliated Germany was faced with political chaos: the navy mutinied in the northern ports while Berlin and Munich were in tumult. Heidegger recognized that the entire prewar way of life—its culture and its bourgeois self-belief—was gone forever. Echoing his belief in phenomenology, he felt nothing was left to him but the "force of personality or belief in the intrinsic value of belonging to the central ego." Yet paradoxically he could not help but feel "a pleasure to be alive," happy that a world that had "merely played with the spirit" was now coming to an end. The future held the promise of a "new era of spirit." Others throughout Germany, imbued with similar spirit, had a different take on affairs. In imitation of Lenin's Bolsheviks in Russia, the south German state of Bavaria declared itself an independent Communist republic. The Spartacists led a revolt in Berlin with the aim of establishing a similar "red republic." Both were soon crushed by the right-wing "Freikorps" (free soldiers), and the Red Terror was followed by a White Terror. Meanwhile the Allied blockade continued, and many began to go hungry.

In 1919, amidst the general despair, Heidegger lost his faith in God. Although he was careful not to inform Husserl, his philosophy was now parting from phenomenology as viewed by its founder. Heidegger was no longer able to accept the transcendental aspects of Husserl's philosophy. He began to consider the transcendental ego as nothing less than an "illusion." The proper study of philosophy should be "the subject which experiences the world," rather than some "bloodless thinking thing which only theoretically thinks the world." The Absolute Being was no longer the aim of Heidegger's phenomenological endeavor. Yet Heidegger's lack of faith should not be mistaken for a simple atheistic view of the world. His outlook remained deeply spiritual: this had always been part of his character and would remain indelibly so. Heidegger initially overcame this anomaly by regarding his philosophy as the form religion takes in "a time of no God." Instead of Absolute Being, the focus of his philosophy would be the study of "being" itself. "What is being?" This would be the central question of his philosophy. Other similar questions open up the different possibilities inherent in this approach. "What is is?" "What precisely do I discover when I think about my own existence?" "What does 'to exist' mean?" The shades of meaning are subtle and shifting. "What does it mean to exist?"

Being would be the replacement for Husserl's pure consciousness, but it was approached in much the same way. The being that Heidegger wished to contemplate was as empty of acts and objects as Husserl's "bracketed out" consciousness. It was the root that lay beyond science, beyond psychology, beyond even logic—beyond all particularity.

Several critics have seen in Heidegger's concept of being a harking back to the ancient idea of the soul. Heidegger initially scorned such "willful misinterpretation." Being was both more and less than the soul. It was grounded in existence. Similarly, it was not individual: like Husserl's "pure consciousness," it lay beyond individual particularities and thus took on a universal aspect. The soul continued beyond existence; but being *was* existence. Despite all his rebuttals, Heidegger's notion of being would at times assume many aspects that had previously been accorded to the soul. As his philosophy developed its more spiritual aspects, it would assume more and more the aspect of a religion without God.

Heidegger turned to the history of philosophy, where he discovered a discernible "history of being." But this had not been a history of progress—on the contrary, it had been an unwitting depiction of loss. The earliest ancient Greek philosophers, known as the pre-Socratics, had reflected deeply on the question of being. Their thought had achieved considerable penetration into this fundamental notion upon which everything rested. But the advent of Socrates, Plato, and Aristotle had been a disaster to such profound and integrated philosophical thought. Under their influence, philosophical thinking had split into separate entities. The attempt to unravel the notion of being had given way to the simple and separate analyses of natural science, political thought, ethics, poetry, and so forth. Meanwhile the core of philosophy had been reduced to ethereal metaphysics. Socrates had claimed that we know nothing. For Plato, the ultimate reality had been ideas. Aristotle had classified nature into different qualities. As a result, the whole notion of being had been overlooked, and over the centuries our understanding of this most fundamental of concepts had become obscured. A gradual "forgetting of being" had occurred, and as a result our notion of "is" had become utterly devalued. What had once been the basis that underlay all philosophy had been reduced to a minor function of grammar. Being, in all its subtlety and depth, had been degraded to a mere copula—"is." A profound mystery had become little more than a verbal glue which held together words in a sentence.

Heidegger sought to restore the profound

mystery to the word "is." This would be done by using a similar method to Husserl's discovery of pure consciousness. Put aside all particular meanings of the copula "is" and you come face to face with the mystery of being.

By forgetting about being, Western philosophy had reduced humanity to a shallowness where it was barely aware of what being meant. It had become oblivious to the properties inherent in the whole notion of being. Modern humanity lived a life devoid of any essential awareness of what its existence meant. Its "beingness" had lost all depth, it no longer had any resonance. Humanity's very knowledge of "beingness" had evaporated amidst a welter of scientific and technological knowledge. Indeed, this was not knowledge at all—just mere "knowhow." In this way, man's beingness itself had become lost to him. Over the centuries, Western philosophy had caused humanity to lose its primeval experience of itself. This "forgetfulness of being" had finally resulted in nihilism and a world dominated by technology. Instead of thinking about being, thinking had been reduced to mere logic, science, technology and the blood-less, beingless metaphysics of post-Socratic philosophy. This had culminated in the age of science—but "science does not think."

What is all this about? Is "is" anything else but what it is? Is being "is" more than being "is being"? Heidegger's contemporary, Wittgenstein, had a similar insight when he remarked: "It is not how things are in the world that is mystical, but *that* it exists." Yet having made this statement, Wittgenstein preferred to remain silent about such things. In his opinion, this was something we simply cannot talk about in language as we know it. Surprisingly, Heidegger concurred with this approach—after his own fashion. It was indeed impossible to talk about such things in the language as it stood. What was needed was an entirely new form of language which would enable us to grasp the elusive nuances evoked by the concept of being. What might have appeared perilously close to nonsense in normal everyday language would now be expressed in an entirely new philosophical jargon expressly invented by Heidegger for the purpose. It would take Heidegger some years to perfect the technical intricacies of this jargon, but he would eventually succeed in arriving at the point where it is all but impenetrable to the uninitiated. For example: "'Nature' as the categorical aggregate of those structures of Being which a definite entity encountered within-the-world may possess, can never make *worldhood* intelligible." I have purposely chosen a more simple example—which can, with effort, be understood. But once it is understood, what precisely *is* understood? Does this kind of verbiage mean anything at all outside itself? Later Heidegger appears to contradict himself with the uncharacteristically clear assertion that "Talking is talk about something." But we must remember that this "about something" is beyond the reach of mere logic. "Being-with belongs to Being-in-the-world, which in every case maintains itself in some definite way of concernful Being-with-one-another." This raises the question of whether meaning itself has any being in such language. Modern philosophers have been far from unanimous in their answer to this problem.

In 1923 Heidegger was appointed associate

professor of philosophy at the small historic university of Marburg in central Germany. He had a growing reputation, but his appointment to a professorship at the comparatively early age of thirty-three was largely due to the influence of Husserl. Heidegger quickly established himself as a cult figure. Phenomenology was very much the latest philosophical craze among the students, and his lectures attracted an avid following.

Heidegger delivered his lectures dressed in south German folk costume: a loden jacket and knickerbockers. This tolerable eccentricity was intended to emphasize the Germanness and "folkish authenticity" of his approach. Here was a man whose being was grounded in the time-honored traditions of the land. During vacations he would retire to the mountains of the Black Forest, living in an Alpine chalet which he had built for himself. (Not literally: all the building work was supervised by his wife, Elfride, in between looking after their two children.) Here amidst plain but far from primitive domesticity, surrounded by the timeless world of unspoiled nature, he could reflect upon the nature of being—high above the shallow corruptions of modern life.

Meanwhile, fewer than seventy miles down the road from Marburg, at the equally historic university of Göttingen, equally incomprehensible speculations were being carried out into the nature of being. The resident physicists, spearheaded by the twenty-five-year-old boy-wonder Werner Heisenberg, were literally inventing the entire field of quantum mechanics. Scientifically, philosophically, politically, and artistically, revolutionary developments were occurring in Germany, where postwar debt was plunging society into the chaos of hyperinflation. (At one point in June 1923, when the bakeries opened in the morning a loaf of bread cost twenty thousand marks; by the time they closed that evening the same loaf cost five *million* marks.) Not surprisingly, artists, philosophers, and scientists were not the only ones who were coming to their own radical conclusions concerning the nature of being.

In 1924 Heidegger became aware of an attractive young Jewish girl attending his lectures. In consequent discussions it soon emerged that despite her evident immaturity, she was by far the most philosophically gifted of his students. This was Hannah Arendt, who came from the East Prussian city of Königsberg. Within weeks their intense philosophical discussions had begun straying into equally obscure and problematic emotional waters. Hannah Arendt was just eighteen and Heidegger was thirty-five when they became lovers. From the wording of Heidegger's letters, it is evident that this was the first time in his life he had experienced full-blown passion—in all its physical, spiritual, and emotional aspects. It was a powerful revelation to him. Before this the repressed young professor in his buttoned-up peasant jacket had characterized himself as possessed of "an inherited reserve and awkwardness." Writing to a colleague he had declared, "I live in solitude"—despite the presence at home of his wife and two growing sons. Although technically both Prussians, Hannah and Heidegger's wife Elfride could not have been more different. Hannah came from a cosmopolitan Jewish family, which was both liberal and assimilated to the German bourgeois way of life. Elfride was descended from the imperially minded and conservative Junker officer caste, a hotbed of racist and German supremacist illusions masquerading as "ideals."

It is clear that with Hannah, Heidegger discovered an entirely new realm of being within himself. This must surely have affected his understanding of "being" and what it meant—yet none of it directly entered his philosophy of being. One can only assume that it informed his vision in a more oblique way. There is no mistaking his feelings. The brittle shell cracked open to reveal the gooey yolk of unfulfilled love. Hannah became everything to him, but most of all she became his muse. Heidegger was in the middle of writing the great work in which he was setting down his original ideas in all their entirety, and his discussions with Hannah of the central points of his philosophy proved an inspiration.

Hannah for her part was overwhelmed with love and admiration for her charismatic master, who was almost twice her age. (My characterization of one as "Hannah" and the other as "Heidegger" is intended to be indicative, not chauvinistic.) But this could be no ordinary love affair. Although Marburg was officially a city, it was in reality a very small provincial town with a population of less than twenty thousand. During university vacations the town virtually closed down. Everybody watched everybody, and the university itself was markedly conservative in its mores—as indeed was the entire German academic tradition, which was highly protective of its social status. By having an affair with a young student, Heidegger was risking not only his job but his entire career—the only time in his life when he ever came near to doing such a thing. Heidegger and Hannah were forced to conduct their affair in the utmost secrecy. His letters filled with complex instructions preceded their every tryst in her attic room. The Alpine uniform was presumably camouflaged beneath a despised urban raincoat. Elfride, who resented all of her husband's female students, was only slightly more suspicious of the "Jewess." Even so, their

secret continued to remain undetected. Just—
there were a number of near scrapes.

But after a year of such nail-biting tension,
Heidegger's nerve gave way. Self-preservation
eventually got the better of his emotions. He sug-
gested to Hannah that she move to Heidelberg to
continue her studies. Hannah dutifully, if regret-
fully, obeyed. They continued to meet on an ir-
regular basis. When he was traveling to deliver a
public lecture at another university, Heidegger
would scheme for a stolen few hours with her at
some village inn. Upon his summons, Hannah
would drop everything and hurry to meet him.
But she was all too aware of what was happening. She began an affair with a fellow student in
the hope of shocking Heidegger into a commit-
ment, but he did not respond as she had hoped.
A few years later she would marry her student
lover. Despite this, Heidegger continued to hold
a central place in her wounded affections. Although he was safely back in his shell, Heidegger
too would never be able to forget what Hannah
had once meant to him. This is more than just
sentimental speculation. Over the years these

remnant feelings would continue to play a crucial if ambiguous role in both their lives.

In 1927 Heidegger finally published the work in which he set down his new philosophy. This was *Being and Time* (in German, *Sein und Zeit*), which he dedicated "to Edmund Husserl, in friendship and admiration." The book opens with a quotation from Plato: "Clearly you have long been aware of what you mean when you use the word 'being.' We, on the other hand, who used to think we understood it, have now become perplexed." Heidegger begins by laying out his argument with extreme care. The point he is trying to establish is slippery in the extreme, and if it is not grasped at the outset the increasingly dense argumentation of the ensuing 480 pages may elude the reader completely. He opens with a series of questions: "Do we in our time have an answer to the question of what we really mean by the word 'being'?" He answers this question with an emphatic no. (In German, *keineswegs*, literally "no ways." This point is important, as Heidegger places great emphasis on the root meaning of words. His intention is to show us a "way through" to the understanding of "being.") Heidegger continues: "Thus it is apt that we should raise once more *the question of the meaning of Being*." The emphasized final phrase is the central notion of the entire book. Even at this early stage we may find ourselves asking, what on earth is he talking about? Does all this mean anything at all? Heidegger was evidently aware that his argument might from the outset provoke such rational responses. He immediately seeks to forestall any dismissive response we might have—by showing that we are missing the point. He continues: "Nowadays are we even perplexed by our inability to understand the word 'Being'?" Once again the answer is an emphatic *keineswegs*.

Unlike Heidegger, many of us are inclined to find nothing puzzling about this concept. We simply accept it for what it is, in a rational manner. We don't attempt to "understand" it in any profound sense: we have no difficulty with it. A thing either has being (that is, it exists) or it does not. A horse exists, a unicorn does not. Although Heidegger does not elaborate, it is worth pointing out that our simple straightforward approach is capable of considerable subtlety—which extends far beyond the rational and the logical. For instance, we can believe God exists, or has "being." We can believe in the possibility that somewhere in the universe another form of intelligent life exists and has its own form of being. We can even produce probability calculations which seek to measure the likelihood of belief in this form of being turning out to be true. Furthermore, the apparently impossible concept of i (the square root of minus one) *exists;* that is, it has "being" mathematically, even though it cannot exist as a number. But Heidegger is not satisfied with this. If we are not perplexed at our understanding of the word "being," we should be. Why are we not perplexed? "First of all we must reawaken an understanding for the meaning of this question." He plainly states the aim of his treatise: "to work out the question of the meaning of being." There is a mystery here, and his intention is to try to see a way through to understanding it.

Central to Heidegger's conception of being is

the word *Dasein*. Put simply, Heidegger means here "human existence." Or, as he elaborates, *Dasein* is "the entity which in its being we know as human life." This is the entity which "in the specificity of its being . . . each one of us is." *Dasein* is the entity "which each one of us finds in the fundamental assertion: I am."

Having cleared up this point, Heidegger emphasizes that the "being" of *Dasein* is its understanding of its own being. In understanding its own being, it simultaneously understands the being of beings which are other than its own being.

At other points he further elaborates the concept of *Dasein*. Fundamentally this is contained in the actual meaning of the word itself, *Da-sein*. Literally "There" (*Da-*) "being" (*-sein*). The essential element of *Dasein* is thus "being-there," or "being-in-the-world." This is our existence, our "mine-ness." It is the "specificity of our being" where "we ourselves are." It is the place where subject encounters object.

Once again, all this prompts the inevitable question. If "talking is talk about something," what is he talking about here? Before dismissing such repetitive verbiage out of hand, it is worth examining what it *does* in fact say. Compare Heidegger's conclusions with the rational clarity of Descartes's fundamental conclusion concerning the human self. Descartes had argued that it was possible to doubt the existence of everything. The entire world and our apprehension of it might be an illusion—but I cannot doubt that I am thinking. Thus: "I think, therefore I am." Despite its apparent transparency, this insight is obscured by its own grammar. Descartes's use of the word "I" is smuggled in by the nature of the verb "to think" and the verb "to be." If we really doubt everything, we in fact conclude that the concept "thinking" inevitably implies the concept "existing." The "I" of this thinking and the "I" of this existing are merely requirements of grammar. On the other hand, Heidegger's *Dasein* reaches beyond the realm of logic, beyond syntax, into the barely graspable ground of our basic intuition. Here Heidegger's conclusion concerning the fundamental apprehension of our existence is deeper and more undeniable than Descartes's. My fundamental apprehension is not "I think, therefore I am" but of my very "being-in-the-world." Admittedly, such a concept has somehow to reach beyond the language that trapped Descartes in its net. Yet whether this requires the obscurities that Heidegger introduced is another matter.

Heidegger argued that the question of being had been ignored for so long precisely because it was so obvious, so close to us, that we literally overlooked it. *Dasein* was too close to be grasped in everyday life, and at the same time lay beyond it. *Dasein* stood behind our empirical questioning of the world, beyond the reach of science. By concentrating on the question of being, it was possible for us to become totally involved in *Dasein*, but we could never avoid everyday existence. "In the moment of vision indeed, and often just 'for that moment,' existence can even gain the mastery over the 'everyday'; but it can never extinguish it."

Heidegger avowed that the aim of his philosophy was to make each individual approach the "question of being" as intensely as possible. Yet our understanding of *Dasein* was inevitably a matter of individual interpretation. This involved unearthing what lay beneath an entire history of misunderstanding. Philosophy had ignored and misinterpreted the question of being. "Being" did not exist in some "higher" realm. It was not metaphysical in this sense. This misapprehension had begun with Plato and continued into the Middle Ages. It had persisted through to Husserl and his concept of Absolute Being, which arose out of a "bracketed out" universally true and pure consciousness. But *Dasein* is categorically different: "being-there" is being-in-the-world, not in some metaphysical beyond. This becomes clear when we concentrate upon *Dasein*.

Yet what precisely does become clear here? Heidegger himself was forced to concede defeat at this point. Finding himself in a time of crisis, he felt that we are not for the present able to reach a precise answer, some truth, about *Dasein*. He would later express this in a poem:

We are too late for the gods
and too early for Being. Being's poem,
just begun, is man.

46

For the time being, all we could do was progress toward *Dasein*. For us, in the present time, the question of being had no answer. The journey was what was important, not the arrival. This was the essential task of thought.

So if for the present there were no answers, what *could* thinking about the question of being produce for us? Only continual "reformulations" of the question of being were possible for us. We could concentrate on the meaning of being, or the truth of being. Alternatively, we could concentrate on the region of being (its location, *where* it existed) or on the very existence of being. All of these could produce an understanding of being. Heidegger characterized this understanding as "disclosedness." This phenomenological method was the letting be seen of what discloses itself. What was disclosed was not immediately apparent, it did not show itself. It was the ground of all that did show itself in the "being-there."

Some may find that "what was disclosed" was not the only thing here that is not immediately apparent. For many who read Heidegger it was not immediately apparent what on earth he was talking about. Heidegger himself was fortunately aware of this difficulty and the need to address it. In order to clarify his thinking at this point, he used a characteristically homely rural metaphor. This method of understanding the question of being, he said, was like cutting a clearing in a wood. We clear the thicket of trees and undergrowth so that light can be shed on the ground of the clearing. The German word *lichtung* means "a clearing"—but it also contains the word *licht,* which means "light." We shed light upon the cleared ground which lies hidden beneath what is immediately apparent. We expose its grounding, which is thus "disclosed."

But even for Heidegger there is a difficulty here. When we disclose being that is concealed, we unconceal it. What is unconcealed he calls *aletheia.* This is the ancient Greek word for "truth"—but it also means unforgetfulness or unconcealment. Yet according to Heidegger, this very unconcealment produces concealment. How can this be so? By unconcealing we disclose being in one way, yet at the same time we conceal all its other possibilities. By choosing one disclosure, we close off the other possible disclosures. This explains how being can have a history, which is not necessarily a history of progress. What the ancient Greeks disclosed of being has now been lost to us in our technological disclosure of being. Our unconcealment has resulted in a concealment.

Here, as in many places, Heidegger's argument goes to the root meaning of words. He relies upon their original meaning to support his argument. But why should the earlier, or ancient, usage of words be in any way superior to modern usage? Heidegger would claim that they have priority. This is true—but only in the strict sense of being prior in time. This can be seen in his use, and misuse, of the word *aletheia*. In ancient Greek this is *a-letheia*—not-forgetfulness, or unconcealment. (The prefix *a* means "not," as in anorexia, meaning literally "no appetite." *Letheia* appears in the River Lethe, the river of forgetfulness, which according to the ancient myth we must all cross after death.) Heidegger argues that the ancient understanding of being has become concealed, or forgotten. But implicit in the Greek word *aletheia* is an entirely erroneous concept of memory. According to Socrates, all knowledge is recollection. Memory simply recovers knowledge that we acquired in its ideal state before birth. (The original meaning of the word "education" derives from this same concept. E-ducate literally means in Latin "to lead out": in other words, to bring out something that is already there. Put another way, according to this notion of education Laurel and Hardy were nuclear physicists waiting to happen.) So according to this ancient concept, memory enables us to reach the truth: *aletheia*—unconcealment, unforgetfulness. But of course we now know that this is not how we acquire knowledge. Going to the root meaning of words, or the resonances of previous meaning that they contain, is no guarantee of arriving at an essential truth. Heidegger is right: buried in words is the history of their meaning. But this history is not necessarily a history of corruption or concealment. On the contrary, the history of a word's *usage*—as distinct from its verbal meaning—is frequently a record of progress toward a truer picture of what actually happens. The Greeks still use the word *aletheia* for "truth." But neither we nor they now regard truth as unforgetfulness (or unconcealment). Why not? Because truth has no necessary link with memory, it is not originally discovered within it. Many of Heidegger's concepts suffer from this defective approach.

By co-opting words for his own purposes (such as *Dasein*), taking old ones out of context (such as *aletheia*), running words together (such as *being-in-the-world*), and so forth, Heidegger managed to create his own inimitable language. This cast a spell over all intelligibility but its own, to-it-self. "We have seen that the world, *Dasein*-with, and existence are *equiprimordially disclosed*; and state-of-mind is a basic existential species of their disclosedness, because this disclosedness itself is essentially being-in-the-world." This is but a minor example, where the being of intelligibility-in-itself hovers at the edge of its own exclusivity. As Heidegger himself so aptly put it: "The Nothing nothings." But does this really get to the bottom of nothing, one wonders. Or is it perhaps nothing-at-all? One must assume that Heidegger is being serious when he warns us with adroit mixed metaphor: "When irrationalism, as the counterplay of rationalism, talks about the things to which rationalism is blind, it does so only with a squint." For Shakespeare "the play's the thing"; for Heidegger play itself manages to talk cross-eyed. As he soberly warns us: "We must avoid uninhibited word-mysticism." An admonition that he immediately follows with: "Nevertheless, the ultimate business of philosophy is to preserve the *force* of the most elemental words in which *Dasein* expresses itself, and to keep the common understanding from leveling them off to that unintelligibility which functions in turn as a source of pseudo-problems." Indeed, even for us of "the common understanding," words that have "force" at the expense of meaning are devoid of pseudo-problems. Instead they have *real* problems if they are to be understood at all.

Heidegger's declared aim was to "determine the essence of man solely in terms of his relationship to being." Such inward-looking exclusiveness reminds us that Narcissus too derives from that era of integrated being which ended with Socrates. It also begs a vital question: what if "the essence of man" lies elsewhere than in the realm of this denatured being? What if it lies in part, or entirely, in the realm of psychology, or social existence, or religion, or political existence, or rational philosophical investigation—or in a fusion of several of these? What if there is no such thing as existence without these particular aspects of it? Indeed, is it possible to conceive at all of existence devoid of such attributes?

In order to come to terms with Heidegger, one must leave aside such quibbles. How are we to arrive at this "essence of man," or at least progress toward it? According to Heidegger, this could be done only by eliminating the accidental and the trivial as we concentrate on the core of human being. Only by the anticipation of death is every accidental and "provisional" possibility driven out. By grasping the "finitude of one's existence," one frees oneself from the shallow "multiplicity of possibilities" that life presents to

53

us. By shunning such things as comfort and the easy life, and by not ignoring the question of death, we can "bring *Dasein* into the simplicity of its *fate*." In angst, or disquieting guilt, or the grim prospect of dying, the being of *Dasein* is disclosed to us. Such extremes are necessary because of the deep fall or decay (*Verfall*) that has occurred in Western thought. *Ver-fall*: literally to "fall away"—man has fallen away from his being. This has been brought about by our exaggerated and one-sided technical development, which ignores our deeper being. (Here it is seemingly necessary to overlook the fact that this development elevated most of us from a nasty, brutish, and short life, giving us the leisure and conditions in which we *could* think about our existence.) At any rate, the result is that we now have "a highly inauthentic way of being."

This inauthenticity has been inevitable to human existence, and has characterized it more or less since Socrates, Plato, and Aristotle ruined everything. According to Heidegger, the curse of inauthenticity comes from simply not concentrating one's life upon the question of being. It occurs in individual behavior, arising from such trivial pursuits as brain surgery, devoting one's life to the selfless service in a leper colony, or becoming a chess grand master. And it occurs in the behavior of an entire epoch, such as the Hellenic period, the Renaissance, and the Enlightenment.

In 1928 Husserl retired from the professorship of philosophy at Freiburg. On his strong recommendation, Heidegger was given the post. At thirty-nine he was now a full professor. His inaugural lecture was entitled "What Is Metaphysics?" In this he further elaborated on his existential philosophy. Once again the young charismatic professor in his homespun mountain peasant's outfit lambasted modern industrialized society. Such a "back to basics" plea found a ready hearing in Germany in 1928. The country was beginning to recover from the ruin of the inflation years, but many solid middle-class citizens had lost all their savings, and with them their status. An undercurrent of deep dissatisfaction remained with the fate of Germany in the twentieth century. The powerful, self-confident nation that the kaiser had led into the world war had within ten years been reduced to an anxious, money-grubbing society ruled by bickering politicians.

In his lecture Heidegger outlined how man's *Verfall* was now leading to his being becoming submerged in his surroundings. His being was becoming a thing. His individuality was becoming lost—to the point where he was becoming, in a very real sense, a nonentity, a nobody. Man was becoming *das Man* (literally "that one," an alien object). Instead of concentrating on his own being, man ignored himself and faced outward. This "other-directedness" meant that he now saw himself in terms of his fellow citizens. Instead of defining himself in his being, he measured himself against his society.

The effects of *das Man* were all too recognizable in modern society. Mass behavior gave rise to mass lives: shallow living begat shallow being. Conversations filled with idle chatter generated no genuine intimacy, and as a result personal relationships were reduced to inauthenticity. Instead of genuine learning, *das Man* was filled with mere "curiosity." He sought out the new rather than the true. Such distractions, the continual search for something different, new fashions—all induced an indifference toward the question of being. The "people" in this mass manifestation sought banal contentment, which was devoid of deep joy. "Knowing joy is the door to the eternal."

Although this was a "time without God," Heidegger's position remained undeniably religious. As the critic A. D. Naess has observed, "The search for Being is merely a disguised quest for a kind of belief in God." Either way, this God—absent or present—had no place in modern life. Heidegger remained insistent upon this point. Modern industrial society produced widespread misery and shallow happiness in equal measure. There was no room for freedom of thought and action, or independence of being in any form. And so Heidegger's misanthropic lament went on, and on ... "all these fads— jazz, Charlie Chaplin, Plato in paperback—a disaster!" Not only would Heidegger have seen *this* book as a disaster, but also the fact that you are reading it. Even though it was about him, this would not have mitigated its deplorableness. Presumably you should have gone to the original German for enlightenment. There you could have come face to face with the genuine article: "Our analysis of the worldhood of the world has constantly been bringing the whole phenomenon of Being-in-the-world into view, although its constitutive items have not all stood out with the same phenomenal distinctness as the phenomena of the world itself." Or, to put it with more deceptive transparency: "When we think of being we arrive at our real home."

In the early 1930s the world was plunged into the Great Depression. Germany's fragile economic recovery collapsed once more. An embittered nation turned to extremes. In April 1933 Hitler and the Nazis came to power. One of the first moves of the Nazi government was to purge the civil service of all Jews. In Germany the universities are part of the civil service. The effect was catastrophic. One example will suffice. The mathematics department at Göttingen, regarded at the time as the world's finest, was led by the aging David Hilbert, one of the greatest mathematicians of his age. When asked by a visiting Nazi minister what he thought of his new "Germanized" mathematics department, Hilbert simply replied: "There is no mathematics department." When even academia was not spared, other realms of society could expect far, far worse. The suicides, and those Jews fortunate enough to flee the country, leaving behind all they possessed, would come to be regarded as the lucky ones.

In May 1933 Heidegger accepted the appointment as rector of Freiburg University, an appointment that required him to become a member of the Nazi party. But this was more than just a case of overweening ambition leading him into dangerous waters. He quickly made his views clear, in his own inimitable style: "The will to the essence of the German university is the will to science as will to the historical mission of the German people as a people that knows itself in its state." In so far as this statement means anything at all, such "will to science" had become a very sorry affair. Germany's great achievements in relativity and nuclear physics, the work of Einstein, Heisenberg (who was not Jewish), and other German Nobel prizewinners, was now dismissed as "Jewish science."

Hannah Arendt wrote to Heidegger, unable to believe what she had heard about her revered philosophic mentor. Heidegger wrote back to her denying any anti-Semitism. Meanwhile he severed all relations with Husserl, who was Jewish and in consequence was dropped as professor emeritus. (Heidegger would also quietly remove the dedication to Husserl from the fourth edition of *Being and Time*.)

Such actions may be indefensible, but do they compromise Heidegger's philosophy? Many commentators, who nonetheless abhor his actions, remain convinced that his behavior here does not affect his philosophy. On the other hand, it seems undeniable that elements of Heidegger's philosophy lead to conclusions that have recognizable echoes in the beliefs of German triumphalism. Take, for instance, his ideas on the language necessary for "genuine philosophizing." It may come as a surprise that someone possessed of Heidegger's way with language had very clear views about its proper use. He was convinced that living philosophy could only be conducted in living language. Latin was a dead language, but its death had affected almost all European languages. Italian, French, Spanish, English—all these derived from the dead language of Latin. This dead language led to dead thinking. Thought in such languages was diverted from the wellspring of being. Just one language remained unaffected by this—German. Only the German language had a direct link going back to ancient Greek, which was the "primordial language"—the original language from which other European languages derived. Thus proper philosophical thinking could only be done in German. This gave the German people a special destiny. "Only from the Germans can world-historical meditation come—provided that they find and defend what is German."

When Heidegger joined the Nazi party, this was more than just careerism: "I saw in the movement that had gained power [the Nazis] the possibility of an inner recollection and renewal of the people and a path that would allow it to discover its historical vocation in the Western world." There is no doubt that his philosophical thinking had led him to this. His rejection of the modern in favor of the "folkish" element of German culture accorded with similar (if more insidious) Nazi ideas about the pure German *volk* (folk). On the other hand, how he squared his abhorrence of mass culture with the behavior at the Nazi Nuremberg rallies quite simply defies plausible explanation. There were, it seems, two types of mass culture: true German culture and "debased" modern American culture.

Living in his ivory tower (or cosy Alpine hut), Heidegger seems to have had little awareness of the full consequences of what he was doing, as well as a considerable amount of wishful thinking. Both the philosopher and his philosophy appear to have favored "bracketing out" certain aspects of reality. *This* is the dangerous and self-delusory aspect of his philosophy that led him to support German resurgence. His philosophy *as such* does not include Nazi ideas.

Further evidence of this self-delusory attitude

is seen in Heidegger's dealings with Hannah
Arendt. In the same letter that he wrote to her
defending himself against the charge of anti-
Semitism, he also appeared to attempt a justifi-
cation of his anti-Semitism. No matter what he
was said to have done, he wrote, this did not affect his personal relationships with Jews—such
as herself, and Husserl. His dealings with
Husserl were a tragic farce. At the same time he
was forced to dismiss his old friend, he ensured
that his wife sent Husserl flowers and a consol-
ing note.

Yet even Heidegger soon found it difficult to
maintain such obfuscation. What could be
achieved in prose was not quite so easy in life. In
his opening address as rector he had spoken of
his hopes for the future. In the words of his biog-
rapher Safranski, "he wished for a return of the
Greek world in the social life of the revolution as
the restoration of the original 'power' of the
'awakening of Greek philosophy.'" But the
"power" and the "philosophy" were now becoming increasingly divergent. His rectorship
carried him into ever more perilous moral waters

as he sought to implement the latest directives from the Nazi ministry of education. Only when he retreated to his Alpine chalet at Todtnauberg in the Black Forest could he remain close to his Greek dream. Below in Freiburg, Nazi thugs roamed the campus. For a while he clung to the belief that "all great things outlast the storm." Then, less than a year after his appointment as rector of his old university, he abruptly resigned.

During the following months there were a number of insulting references to him in Nazi magazines, but there was no danger of him losing his post as professor of philosophy. He remained a member of the party. At one stage there was even talk of him being appointed director of the Prussian Academy of Professors, but he was glad when this fell through. It would have meant him moving to Berlin. He remained very much a philosopher who was rooted to place—constantly fulminating against "powerless and bottomless thinking." Again according to Safranski: "Heidegger's faith in Hitler and the need for revolution was unbroken." Even so, he gradually began to distance himself from politics. "His philosophy had sought a hero, and it had been a political hero. But now he was once more separating the spheres." Philosophy was "deeper" than politics. Being was the driving spirit of events, but it did not have to become absorbed in them. As was so often the case, it became increasingly difficult to distinguish between Being in general and Heidegger's individual being.

With the approach of the inevitable war, he gradually withdrew into himself. As the darkness of war descended, "philosophy . . . as a structure of culture" became all but superfluous, surviving only as a "being-addressed by Being itself." Even so, in the midst of World War II he was still willing to make pronouncements: "Today we know that the Anglo-Saxon world of Americanism is determined to destroy Europe, and thus our homeland, and thus the origin of the Occidental." Everything had to be seen in terms of "destiny." Aggrandizement justified all. Heidegger's own personal being became Being, Germany's "fate" became the Fate of Western Civilization, no less. The fact that France, Britain, by then much of Italy, and even his beloved Greece were fighting alongside the Americans (who included soldiers descended from all European nations, and were led by a man with the unmistakably German name of Eisenhower) does not seem to have occurred to him. Only Germany could now apparently lay claim to the "origin of the Occidental."

1945 left Germany and all such thinking in ruins. Heidegger was stripped of his post at the university. Meanwhile his house, together with his precious library, were requisitioned by the occupying French forces. Heidegger was outraged and wrote to the military authorities: "I wish to protest in the strongest possible terms against this attack on my person and on my work. Why should I have been singled out for punishment and defamation before the eyes of the whole city—indeed before the eyes of the world?" He still did not understand. Yet worse was to come. He now had to suffer the "indignity" of appearing before a denazification committee to explain himself. Even so, he still saw no reason to assume "personal responsibility" for his public support for the führer. As a consequence, he was banned from teaching—a ban that would last until 1951. But he still covertly lectured to private gatherings of well-heeled citizens, many of whose feelings toward the immediate past remained as ambiguous as his own. He had not personally been responsible for anti-Semitic atrocities, and one assumes that the revelations of the Holocaust must have horrified him. Yet still he refused to apologize. And thus it would remain.

In 1968 Heidegger invited the great German-Jewish poet Paul Celan for a three-day visit to his chalet at Todtnauberg. Heidegger deeply admired the angst-ridden quality of Celan's poetry: reading it was to approach the question of being. Likewise Celan had long deeply admired Heidegger's thought and was warmly welcomed by the aging philosopher—one of the few to be honored with an invitation to stay with him at Todtnauberg. The two men were utterly disparate: the quiet, private, admiring old man, and the mentally unstable poet obsessed with the fate of his people. Surprisingly, they appeared to achieve a deep rapport. Yet even then no apology was forthcoming. Celan left, utterly bewildered.

Some years earlier Heidegger had been visited by Hannah Arendt. By now she had a growing reputation in America as a political philosopher, though her thinking remained deeply influenced by Heidegger. Before their first postwar meeting she was wary of him—naturally suspicious of his attitude and stance during the Nazi era. Yet face to face it all seemed different: something of their former intellectual intimacy rekindled. She was happily married, and Heidegger had told Elfride about his earlier affair with Hannah. Elfride, who remained anti-Semitic, grudgingly accepted Hannah's presence during their subsequent meetings when Hannah visited Europe.

Hannah Arendt did her best to promote Heidegger's work in America, ensuring that his ideas were understood and appreciated among a wider audience. Heidegger's reputation gradually emerged from under its cloud, and his influence began to spread. For years he had already been appreciated in Europe—most notably by the

French existentialist Jean-Paul Sartre. But now, with the publication of the English translation of *Being and Time* in 1962, he was assured of a worldwide reputation.

A year later Hannah Arendt reported on the Jerusalem trial of the Nazi war criminal Adolf Eichmann. In the course of this, she coined the phrase "the banality of evil" to describe Eichmann, whose bureaucratic small-mindedness had been responsible for such unspeakable horror. Although she refused to admit it, she had already encountered a man whose behavior fitted this category. Arendt remained a deep admirer of Heidegger, sometimes to the point of self-delusion. Heidegger, for his part, never fully accepted Arendt's growing fame.

In 1975 Hannah Arendt died. A year later Heidegger died on May 26, at the age of eighty-six. He was buried, as he had wished, at Messkirch in the Black Forest, where he had been born. Safranski tellingly closes his great biography of Heidegger by quoting the philosopher's own words, used in another context: "Yet once more a way of doing philosophy sinks into the darkness."

Comments and Criticisms

Heidegger specifically quotes several examples of the pre-Socratic thought that he sought to emulate and resurrect:

"... but you should learn all:

the untrembling heart of unconcealment, well-rounded,

and also the opinions of mortals

who lack the ability to trust what is unconcealed."

—Parmenides

In the following passage Heidegger speaks of the concealment of being which aletheia (uncealedness) penetrates to discover the truth of being:

71

Concealment can be a refusal or merely a dissembling. We are never completely sure whether it is one or the other. Concealment conceals and dissembles itself. This means that the open place in the midst of beings, the clearing, is never a precise stage with a permanently raised curtain where the play of beings unfolds. On the contrary, the clearing takes place only as this double concealment. The unconcealment of beings—such is never a simply existent state, instead it is a happening. Unconcealment (truth) is neither an attribute of matters in the sense of beings, nor one of propositions.

—*The Origin of the Work of Art*

Philosophy remains latent in every human existence and need not be first added to it from somewhere else.

—*The Metaphysical Foundations of Logic*

Philosophy gets under way only by a peculiar insertion of our own existence into the fundamental possibilities of Dasein as a whole. For this insertion three things are of decisive importance.

First, we must allow space for beings as a whole. Second, we must release ourselves into the nothing; in other words, we must liberate ourselves from those idols everyone has before which everyone cringes. And finally, we must let the sweep of our suspense take its full course so that it swings back into the basic question of metaphysics which the nothing itself compels: why is there being at all, and why not rather nothing?

—*What Is Metaphysics?*

The greatness of the discovery of phenomenology lies not in results obtained by factual means, which can be evaluated and analyzed and nowadays have certainly evoked a veritable transformation in questioning and working, but rather in this: *it is the discovery of the very possibility of doing research in philosophy.* But a possibility is properly understood in its most proper sense only when it continues to be taken as a possibility and preserved as a possibility. However, preserving it as a possibility does not mean to fix a chance state of research and inquiry as ultimately real and to allow it to solidify; on the contrary, it means to keep open the tendency toward the matters themselves.

—*History of the Concept of Time: Prolegomena*

Hence Being-in is not to be explained ontologically by some ontical characterization, as if one might say, for example, that Being-in in a world is a spiritual property, and that man's "spatiality" is a result of his bodily nature (which, at the same time, always gets founded upon corporeality). Here again we are faced with the Being-present-at-hand-together of some such spiritual Thing with a corporeal Thing, while the Being of the entity thus compounded remains more obscure than ever.

—*Being and Time*

The critical reception of such work was mixed. The celebrated European thinker George Steiner regards Heidegger highly:
... The Heideggerian revaluation ... literally forces one to attempt to rethink the very concept of thought. Only a major thinker can provoke so creatively.

In this context it is worth noting that Steiner is not only Jewish but also well aware of Heidegger's disgraceful behavior during the Nazi era. He also said:

In the history of Western thought [there is] no other work like *Sein und Zeit*.

While many agree with this, not all see such estimation as a complimentary assessment. Other well-known thinkers have been more forthright in their critical opinions. The following is just one example of many, and far from being the most extreme:

The master of complicated banalities. . . . Heidegger's *modus philosophandi* is neurotic through and through and is ultimately rooted in his psychic crankiness. His kindred spirits, close or distant, are sitting in lunatic asylums, some as patients, some as psychiatrists on a philosophical rampage. . . . For all its critical analysis, philosophy has not yet managed to root out its psychopaths. What do we have psychiatric diagnosis for?

—C. G. Jung

Chronology of Significant Philosophical Dates

6th C B.C.	The beginning of Western philosophy with Thales of Miletus.
End of 6th C B.C.	Death of Pythagoras.
399 B.C.	Socrates sentenced to death in Athens.
c 387 B.C.	Plato founds the Academy in Athens, the first university.
335 B.C.	Aristotle founds the Lyceum in Athens, a rival school to the Academy.

324 A.D.	Emperor Constantine moves capital of Roman Empire to Byzantium.
400 A.D.	St. Augustine writes his *Confessions*. Philosophy absorbed into Christian theology.
410 A.D.	Sack of Rome by Visigoths heralds opening of Dark Ages.
529 A.D.	Closure of Academy in Athens by Emperor Justinian marks end of Hellenic thought.
Mid-13th C	Thomas Aquinas writes his commentaries on Aristotle. Era of Scholasticism.
1453	Fall of Byzantium to Turks, end of Byzantine Empire.
1492	Columbus reaches America. Renaissance in Florence and revival of interest in Greek learning.
1543	Copernicus publishes *On the Revolution of the Celestial Orbs*, proving mathematically that the earth revolves around the sun.

1633	Galileo forced by church to recant heliocentric theory of the universe.
1641	Descartes publishes his *Meditations*, the start of modern philosophy.
1677	Death of Spinoza allows publication of his *Ethics*.
1687	Newton publishes *Principia*, introducing concept of gravity.
1689	Locke publishes *Essay Concerning Human Understanding*. Start of empiricism.
1710	Berkeley publishes *Principles of Human Knowledge*, advancing empiricism to new extremes.
1716	Death of Leibniz.
1739–1740	Hume publishes *Treatise of Human Nature*, taking empiricism to its logical limits.
1781	Kant, awakened from his "dogmatic slumbers" by Hume, publishes *Critique of Pure Reason*.

Great era of German metaphysics begins.

1807   Hegel publishes *The Phenomenology of Mind*, high point of German metaphysics.

1818   Schopenhauer publishes *The World as Will and Representation*, introducing Indian philosophy into German metaphysics.

1889   Nietzsche, having declared "God is dead," succumbs to madness in Turin.

1921   Wittgenstein publishes *Tractatus Logico-Philosophicus*, claiming the "final solution" to the problems of philosophy.

1920s   Vienna Circle propounds Logical Positivism.

1927   Heidegger publishes *Being and Time*, heralding split between analytical and Continental philosophy.

1943   Sartre publishes *Being and Nothingness*, advancing

Heidegger's thought and instigating existentialism.

1953   Posthumous publication of Wittgenstein's *Philosophical Investigations*. High era of linguistic analysis.

Chronology of Heidegger's
Life and Times

1889	Martin Heidegger born September 26 in Messkirch in southern Germany.
1909	Studies theology at Freiburg.
1911	Shifts to studying philosophy.
1913	Graduates at Freiburg.
1914	Outbreak of world war.
1917	Marries Elfride Petri.
1918	Heidegger called to active service, but German army collapses before he becomes engaged in

	fighting. Kaiser flees to Holland. Germany surrenders to the Allies.
1920s	Germany hit by the "inflation years." Reichmarks lose their value to the extent that it takes a wheelbarrow full of notes to buy a loaf of bread.
1923	Heidegger becomes associate professor of philosophy at University of Marburg.
1924	Meets and falls in love with eighteen-year-old Hannah Arendt.
1927	Publishes *Sein und Zeit* (*Being and Time*).
1928	Succeeds Husserl as professor of philosophy at University of Freiburg.
1929	Wall Street collapse.
1930s	The Great Depression spreads throughout the world, destroying Germany's fragile economic recovery.

1933	Hitler and the Nazis come to power in Germany. Nazis issue decree dismissing all Jews from the civil service (which includes the universities). Heidegger becomes rector of University of Freiburg.
1934	Resigns as rector.
1939	Outbreak of World War II.
1945	German defeat by Allies.
1945–1951	Heidegger banned from teaching because of Nazi involvement.
1950	Meets Hannah Arendt for the first time since her emigration to America.
1962	English translation of *Being and Time* published.
1976	Dies at the age of eighty-six.

Recommended Reading

Elzbieta Ettinger, *Hannah Arendt / Martin Heidegger* (Yale University Press, 1995). A rare piece of scholarship which goes into considerable detail about the long and difficult relationship between Heidegger and his brightest pupil. A fascinating book, deeply illuminating of both characters.

Charles B. Guignon, ed., *The Cambridge Companion to Heidegger* (Cambridge University Press, 1993). A collection of essays covering all the major topics in Heidegger's philosophy. Difficult but worth the effort.

Martin Heidegger, *Being and Time,* trans. by John Macquarrie and Edward Robinson (Harper & Row, 1962). Heidegger's long and all but impenetrable masterpiece. Readers who start at the beginning and emerge at the other end with their mind intact can count themselves full-fledged philosophers of a high order.

Martin Heidegger, *An Introduction to Metaphysics,* trans. by Ralph Manheim (Yale University Press, 1959). The best introduction to the master's thought and jargon. Comparatively short but nonetheless heavy going.

Hugo Ott, *Martin Heidegger: A Political Life* (Basic Books, 1993). A comprehensive attempt to get to the bottom of Heidegger's controversial political activities during the Nazi years and afterward. An illuminating philosophical morality tale in all shades of grey.

Rüdiger Safranski, *Martin Heidegger: Between Good and Evil* (Harvard University Press, 1998). The most recent and by far the best biography, containing a good balance between life and ideas, and confronting many of the difficulties in both.

George Steiner, *Martin Heidegger* (University of Chicago Press, 1991). A largely sympathetic brief treatment that covers most of Heidegger's fundamental ideas, by the one English-speaking European scholar perhaps most qualified to judge.

M.H. dropped out of Nazi party 6 mths before Hitler took power, see Steiner

Index